Kevin's Favorite Verses For

Summer Days

by Kevin Ahern

DavinciPress Publishers
Corvallis, Oregon

Kevin's Favorite Verses For

Summer Days

Table of Contents

June Twenty First
1529
Queen Catherine of England
After a big stunt was pulled
Tried to get her marriage
To Henry unannulled

Ham soup is an add hock meal

Short Stops
Little Leaguers
At the platter
Each of them
A peanut batter

Shhhh
Undiscovered species
In the ocean cause me fits
I guess it's safe to say it has
An awful lot of sea crits

Drug Cattict
They tranquilized
My cat to spay
So now it is
A slow mews day

Winnabuygo
A motor home
Is really great
An investment in
Wheel estate

Buzz Off
Bees allergic to pollen
Do not have shortened lives
The only effect it seems to have
Is they come down with hives

June Twenty Second
1868
After their secession
Met with no success
The Confederate state of Arkansas
Went and re-joined the U.S.

"You're my rock" is a polite way of saying "I take you for granite"

<u>Clothes Line</u>
The nun most clearly
Explained to the abbott
Her prayers in the shower
Were done out of habit

<u>Under Where?</u>
When Hanes sued Fruit of the Loom
In the underwear market space
The judge decided it quickly
'Twas a very brief case

<u>He Ain't Heavy</u>
When measuring heavy things
The units are up to you
Pounds or kilos, I don't care
Either weigh will do

<u>Copy That?</u>
Xerox bought Wurlitzer
Said JP Morgan
And now they make
Reproductive organs

<u>Spacey</u>
The space alien opera
Is lots of fun
I hear they call it
Aria 51

Kevin's Favorite Verses For Summer Days

June Twenty Third
1960
It changed the world
For Jack and Jill
When the U.S. began selling
The birth control pill

Caching a Cold
I do not like the cold
It's summer I prefer
As far as I'm concerned
It's the month of Decembrrrrr

Wet Head
A rain drop got in trouble
And everybody knew it
Because he partied late last night
I knew he'd overdew it

The Solution
To give your car
A chemical sheen
You're gonna need
Mercedes Benzene

Grave Robber?
They handed me a donor card
For organs, when I depart
The guy who gave it to me
Was after my own heart

Pulling Your Egg
I started a matchmaking service
For chickens, what a feat!
What were my thoughts in doing so?
Just making hens meet

June Twenty Fourth
1916
Because of the fans
That she would attract
Mary Pickford's the first actress
With a million dollar contract

Long bikes are really wonderful

Urban Legoland
A plane crashed into Legoland
And everyone's annoyed
Cuz many thousand square blocks
Immediately were destroyed

Breakfast of Champions
His exercise is going swell
That lazy yuppie goon
He does his crunches twice a day
Cap'n in the morning / Nestle in the afternoon

Taking a Dive
For politicians I provide
This offer that's unmatched
Free bungee jumps for all of them
And there's no strings attached

Untweetable
My bird is dead
Not a peep
Now for sale
Won't go cheep

Waiting Game
The clerk at Legoland
Is off the clock
So customers now
Are lined up for blocks

Kevin's Favorite Verses For Summer Days

June Twenty Fifth
1951
The prettiest thing
You ever did see
The very first broadcast
Of color TV

Over the Hill
That milk for old folks
Made me whine
Because they named it
Pasture Prime

Numbers Game
The doctor said my problem was
Much worse than tendonitis
The problem he referred to as
A case of elevendonitis

A Place to Park
I own a quarry down the road
It is so very fine
But now it's paved and cars park there
I've got a lot on my mine

Talking Smack
I hope you do not get upset
But there's a major issue
If you are not combobulated
Then I am here to dis you

Toon Swoon
When I act Goofy
You can tell
That I am having
A Disney spell

June Twenty Sixth
1963
JFK In West Berlin
Trying to out-reach
Says "I'm a jelly donut"
In a famous speech

Life Saver
A doctor at the painting show
Was truly one fast mover
To the person choking bad she gave
The Guggenheimlich Maneuver

Assembly Required
A UFO lands
And tension increases
It says, "We're from IKEA"
"And we come in pieces"

Looking Buff
The retired nudist
Wrinkly white
Down at the beach
Gets much hindsight

Photo Finish
Dental x-rays
Get teeth fixed
It seems they are
Just tooth pics

One Lump or Two?
Lipton has a product new
I don't think it's for me
It's said to make you worry more
The name? "Anxietea"

Kevin's Favorite Verses For Summer Days

June Twenty Seventh
1955
In Illinois
The public saw
The very first
Seat belt law

Cinemanic
I'm a fan of Robin Williams
His humor I desire
My favorite movie, without a Doubt
Is the classic "Mrs. Fire"

Wild Life
The Serengeti
For a lark
Is what I call
Giraffic Park

Instrumental
The music store thief
Didn't shoot
But went and made off
With the lute

O Canada!
I heard a story yesterday
That I cannot believe
It claims that Canada isn't real
It's only mapleleaf

Alphabetical Order
Old phonograph records had two sides
Known as the "As" and "Bs"
I guess it's apt they got replaced
By things we call "CDs"

June Twenty Eighth
1935
It was better than keeping
Gold in a box
FDR mandates
A vault at Fort Knox

Canadians have Type Eh personalities

Hair Don't
When asked to remove his man bun
The aging hipster said
"I can't believe you said that"
"Knot off the top of my head"

Fur in Hide?
In London, stray beagles wandering 'round
Get caught, as best they can
Because it's metric, all get stored
Inside dog kilograms

Caf-fiend
For fighting off
Sleeping's gods
Coffee helps you
Beat the nods

Socket To Me
That mechanic keeps
The waitress guessing
Will he get salad
With wrench dressing?

Fire Arm
My tattoo artist caused a scare
'Twas unexpected, see?
Because this guy just now has gone
And drawn a gun on me

Kevin's Favorite Verses For Summer Days

June Twenty Ninth
1964
The Civil Rights Act
Finally passes muster
After an 83 day
Filibuster

<u>Sound of Silence</u>
The doctor's message
Was my worst fear
She said I was deaf
'Twas difficult to hear

<u>Wink, Wink</u>
My friend was injured on the job
By safety glasses, see
He poked his cornea with them bad
It was great eyerony

<u>Astro Not</u>
An astronautical space suit
Is worn by big and small
Protecting from exposure to
Literally, nothing at all

<u>Cleaning Up</u>
The Millennium Falcon's clean up crew
Makes traveling much nicer
I hear their work's accomplished with
A good Han sanitizer

<u>Old Ages</u>
That history teacher
Goes on and on
Just why does she
Babylon?

June Thirtieth
1908
The Tunguska fireball
A Siberian mystery
The greatest meteor
In recorded history

With avian disease, it's the early worm that gets the bird

<u>A Peeling</u>
A lady at the swimming pool
Is sure a big praise earner
Because she took her sunscreen out
And put it on the back burner

<u>Higher Power</u>
The Alaskans had some
Gods for sure
And all of them were
Aleutians of grandeur

<u>20-20</u>
My optometrist
Who plays the harp
Says her favorite key
Is C-sharp

<u>Conundrum</u>
If they boldly go where no one has gone
Through galaxies everywhere
How is it possible the Star Trek crew
Encounters someone there?

<u>Stir Fried</u>
An Asian chef most every night
Does something rather shocking
It seems he stands up in his bed
And then begins sleep wokking

Kevin's Favorite Verses For Summer Days

July First
1963
Reflecting that
The U.S. growed
The Postal Service
Started Zip Code

July Thoughts

The month begins with fireworks loud
Those pops and rocket sights
And people shouting out, "Oh wow"
For lovely summer nights

The month will surely go by fast
With people relocating
Our town will empty, then at last
The summer we've awaited

But peace is lost with auto noise
From mufflers loud and grating
Some say they're toys for little boys
Just overcompensating

But you will not hear me attack
These autos I've deplored
Cuz I remember this one fact
A pen is mightier than a Ford

Before I go, vacation's here
Goodbye to winter's glooms
And when your motor home's in gear
You're driving three bed-varooms

<u>Kevin's Favorite Verses For Summer Days</u>

July Second
1937
Even today
We find it weird
That Amelia Earhart
Disappeared

Look at Me
The library's mirror
Is all about
Letting people
Self-check out

Out Standing in his Field
They say it always could be worse
And I'm a big believer
Consider Oz's scarecrow who
Has come down with hay fever

Life Story
So many things I need to do
And it just seems to me
That my to-do list really is
An "ought-to" biography

Extra Crunchy
Octopuses
Crave a dish
Of peanut butter
And jellyfish

Bad Words
I hope you don't find
My thinking subversive
But expletives usually
Are written in "cursive"

July Third
1962
An amazing man
Who changed the game
Jackie Robinson inducted
By the Hall of Fame

Ibuprofanity - what you say when your Advil doesn't work

Big Hooters
Peruvian owls are marvelous
With many attributes
But I think they are just some birds
That really are Inca hoots

Shell Game
My mother has a delivery man
A wonderful guy, but a klutz
He brings her cashews every day
She says he drives her nuts

Lighten Up
When Noah built the ark back then
It was a glorious sight
He saw for miles and miles from it
Thanks to its big flood lights

Bestie Bessie
A noteworthy cow
On the prairie
Is said to be
Legend dairy

Supply-Side Economics
When Swedes fill up
A winter home
They suffer from
Stock home syndrome

July Fourth
1895
"America the Beautiful"
Describes a great view
And on this day
Made its debut

Crafty inmates are put in "You Knit" cells

Give a Dime
Take it from
The old guy, Devin
Change in the air
Means pennies from heaven

Frogman
If a smidgeon Polish
Is your role
I'd say you're just
A tad pole

The Vision Thing
My rear view mirror disappeared
'Twas taken by some hack
But I have gotten over it
And now I don't look back

Litter-ally
In my new work, I'm collecting trash
As I sing a happy song
There was no training required of me
I picked it up as I went along

Roamin' Candle
I do not know the story's source
Of poor old Mr. Smith
Who drank a fifth July the fourth
And couldn't go forth July the fifth

Kevin's Favorite Verses For Summer Days

July Fifth
1942
His James Bond books
Would later tantalize
Ian Fleming graduates
From a training school for spies

Do pennies from heaven mean change is in the air?

New Prayers

Eater
Now I lay me
Down to sleep
Last night I had
Too much to eat
If I should not
Tomorrow wake
It's cuz I got
A stomach ache

Drinker
Now I lay me
Down, I think
I may have had
Too much to drink
If I should moan
Before I wake
Please bring me aspirin
For heaven's sake

My Dog

My dog likes getting table scraps
She eats them with aplomb
I think it would be healthier if
She ate them with a plum

July Sixth
1957
This is the day
That started it all
When Beatle John met
A young man named Paul

Samuel Morse dashed off many letters

New Prayers

<u>Tired</u>

Now I lay me
On my bed
I'm feeling like
The walking dead
If I should snore
And moan and squeak
Please let me sleep
Another week

<u>Tall</u>

Now I lay me
Tween my sheets
Where all is warm
Except my feets
This wish could not
Be any stronger
So please buy sheets
A little longer

Beetles

The most numerous species on the Earth
Are said to be the beetles
To fit them in, for what it's worth
Each one must be quite leetle

Kevin's Favorite Verses For Summer Days

July Seventh
1928
The craziest thing
Anyone had seen
Bread that was sliced
By a machine

<u>Hail Caesar!</u>
The Roman numerals class I aced
Is one that I adore
I just received my grade of 'C'
It was a perfect score!

<u>Razor's Edge</u>
Though now they all
Are roadway ghosts
Burma shave signs
Were once smile posts

<u>Anode That Before I Went</u>
I went to my doc for lithium
This woman is the best
Before she would prescribe it, though
I needed a battery of tests

<u>Interesting</u>
I wrote a verse about my debt
Last evening as I drank
The title for it has been set
It's called "Ode to my Bank"

<u>In the Sticks</u>
Carving wood
Into a fiddle
Works best when done
Whittle by whittle

July Eighth
1913
Alfred Carlton Gilbert
A name you won't forget
Received a patent on this day
For his Erector Set

The worst part of the job for carpet installers is tacks time

Take a Number
My friend's a gynecologist
And everyone assumes
The line of patients that she has
Is called the waiting wombs

Fudging It
The ice cream parlor offered me
A real good job today
I turned it down, because, you see
I do not work on sundaes

Righting Writing
When prose is bad
And rather terse
You know that it
Could be verse

Run Down
Slum lords, wow
How do they sleep?
Making premises
They don't keep

H-2-Uh-Oh
My water pistol didn't work
And I am really pissed
Because when I tried shooting it
The truth is I just mist

Kevin's Favorite Verses For Summer Days

July Ninth
1956
Known as the eternal teenager
Dick Clark knew the bands
He started on this very day
Hosting American Bandstand

The guy who complained about the hot dogs was an Oscar Mayer whiner

String Along
A bathing suit
For veggies teeny
Might be known as
A zucchini

High Tax Bracket
A marijuana grower
Reports what he earns
By the filing of
Joint tax returns

Driven to Drink
My sympathetic friend's for you
Her empathy's appealing
Please tell your plight to her, not me
I have mixed drinks about feelings

No Charges Filed
The word at the hospital
Is everyone talked
A defibrillator broke
And no one was shocked

Frigid Error
When asked about puns on air conditioners
By my buddy Dan
I shook my head at him and said,
"Sorry, not a fan"

July Tenth
1040
Raising awareness of high taxes
Something everybody knows
Lady Godiva rode on horseback
Devoid of all her clothes

Mansplaining is correctile dysfunction

Chips

They planted chips in my vaccine
To see the things I'm seein'

My wife, my kids, the corner bar
My dirty clothes and messy car

My breakfast eggs, my luncheon meat
My closest friends, the things I Tweet

My kitchen and the dining room
The folks in meetings that I Zoom

And when they saw what I'm about
The chips all asked to be let out

Armadillo Love Song

Here's to the armadillo
Strange creature on the road
With armor on the outside
A most protective mode

A love song to this organism
I've with this verse bestowed
So you can go tell all your friends
You've heard an armadillode

Kevin's Favorite Verses For Summer Days

July Eleventh
1804
The most famous U.S. duel
That ever would occur
Took place when Mister Hamilton
Was killed by Aaron Burr

The Romaine empire fell when Brutus kaled Caesar

Doing Business
On the toilet my cat
Is strange for sure
That's where he reads
His litterature

Hard Lesson
The driveway gave me
Some gestault
When I skinned a knee
My dumb asphalt

Armor All
About the medieval period
We've gained some new insights
They called it the dark ages
For having so many knights

Flotation Devices
I like the phrase that it is claimed
One astronaut has said
"That stuff in anti-gravity books"
"Goes up way o'er my head"

No Whey
"Cottage cheese," I blurted out
To friends surprisingly
Then, to address their puzzlement
I said, "It's just a curd to me"

<u>Kevin's Favorite Verses For Summer Days</u>

July Twelfth
1957
Surgeon General Burney
Came up with an answer
Declaring that smoking
Is a cause of lung cancer

<u>Stick It To Them</u>
I note right here, a sporting thing
That I am sad about
I went to the fights the other day
And a hockey game broke out

<u>Slanted I's</u>
I took a course on italics
But felt quite out of place
I flunked it and they tell me that
'Twas cuz I made straight A's

<u>Second Ham</u>
The littlest pig
Has got a frown
His clothing's all
Ham me down

<u>No Slouch</u>
Quasimodo retired today
His pension is a plum
He got 10 years of back pay
And a very large lump sum

<u>Well Grounded</u>
When I opened bills
It made me talk
Water and electric
Gave me a shock

July Thirteenth
1865
Horace Greeley
Had a plan
Declaring to all
"Go west, young man"

The route to the porch light was passed on by word of moth

A Very Famous Restaurant

Into a famous restaurant
I went the other day
Their food is celebrated
Yes, that is safe to say

The **Eydie Gormé** menu
Is what you order from
These were the things I saw on it
I'm hungry, yummy yum

I recommend a tasty dish
If you are feeling pallid
It has a ton of greens and stuff
Their great **Sid Caesar Salad**

If breakfast food's what you desire
The best that you will get
Is served up Rocky Mountain style
The **John Denver Omelette**

An alternative to think about
Should omelettes be the dregs
Is getting just a simple meal
Of **Kevin Bacon and Eggs**

To go with any eggs you get
A great choice, goodness sakes!
Is ordering up there for yourself
A **Robert Stack** of pancakes

July Fourteenth
1938
Howard Hughes
Working day and night
Set a new record
For around the world flight

The bust of Julius Caesar was a head of its time

A Very Famous Restaurant

Vegetables balance diets well
A fact you surely know
I recommend a bit of starch
Edgar Allen Poe-tatoes

Along those lines, remember that
You need more than protein
So don't forget to get yourself
Some tasty **Lorne Green Beans**

Another quite good veggie goes
With several kinds of hams
That would, of course, be what they call
Their famous **John Candied Yams**

"Supplement your food with carbs"
My dietician said
And they have got a yummy choice
Their **Doris Day Old Bread**

Should sandwiches be what you crave
This one will be a joy
The house's spooky specialty
The **Edgar Allen Poe Boy**

The fish they have is rather good
As you're sure to find out
If you should get an order of
Their **Veronica Lake Trout**

Kevin's Favorite Verses For Summer Days

July Fifteenth
1898
The Italian Camilio Golgi
Examining cells quite thin
Discovered the cell apparatus
That was named for him

Birds like to go on pecknics

Fold It Up
Origami love
Is never ceasing
In fact, I'd say that
It's in creasing

Net Gain
Aussie nerds
Are computer wonders
Because they're from
A LAN down under

Sour Drapes
When the venetian blinds salesperson
Got fired, it's for sure
The boss explained clearly
It was curtains for her

Puzzle
Would someone please tell me
Just why it is so
When I ask what IDK means
Everyone says, "I don't know"

Frozen Comments
There are gelato places
Around most everywhere
I like that quite a bit because
They talk desserty to me there

July Sixteenth
1951
He was a recluse
We don't know why
J.D. Salinger
Published "Catcher in the Rye"

Seamstresses have sewnar

Frito Dorito
Doritos are geometric food
Three sided orange spangles
My teacher likes to say they are
I-salsa-les triangles

Very Earie
I cross exotic species
It is a most odd job
One-horn creatures crossed with maize
Give unicorn on the cob

Urine Trouble
A German doctor I know well
Is a kidney specialist
Or as they say in Heidelberg
A real Eurologist

Big Bang
Demolition experts
I should mention
Have a blast
At their conventions

Flipping It
The sports reporting
Had one fault
When the gymnast failed
It was not her vault

Kevin's Favorite Verses For Summer Days

July Seventeenth
1070
Perhaps 'twas because
Of all his name's slanders
That Arnulf the Hapless
Became the Earl of Flanders

<u>On the Clock</u>
Meetings yield
The oddest thoughts
Minutes are kept
But hours are lost

<u>Tall Tale</u>
My autobiography rejection
Caused me tremendous strife
But what about it can I say?
The story of my life

<u>Kinky</u>
My advice to divers shopping is
Beware of eating trends
And when you make rice purchases
Try not to get the Ben's

<u>Quality Control Freak</u>
My buddy's new job at the factory
Is really very sweet
He works there making window shades
Pulls down one K per week

<u>Silent Treatment</u>
A neighbor's dog is barking loud
My patience, wearing thin
Believe me, if I could I would
Give a yappin-dectomy to him

July Eighteenth
1938
"Wrong Way" Corrigan was going to California
But did not know which way to head
And then 28 hours later
He landed in Ireland instead

When you work in a hay field, you bail before you quit

Diet Drug

I went on a diet to drop some weight
So it was most carefully that I ate
At first I thought it would be great

I ate salads light with calories low
Most anxious for the weight to go
And ready for the scales to show

I pumped some iron and ran around
But to my chagrin, I quickly found
I hadn't lost a single pound

I went to my doc and asked her views
For dieting, did she have clues?
That's when she shared disturbing news

It seems I'd done the diet right
And though I'd tried with all my might
It was a rather hopeless fight

Because the weight that I'd accrued
From eating too much tasty food
Had been securely Super Glued

So listen to me, hear my roar
If dieting's what you abhor
Then try my brand new, Stick-No-More™
Available in your local store

Kevin's Favorite Verses For Summer Days

July Nineteenth
1799
The key to hieroglyphics
Was found in a village today
The Rosetta stone made possible
What we know of old language today

Heard Immunity
To vaccinated friends, I tried
Relating a joke I'd sweated
It was about the measles, but
It seems they didn't get it

Havana Other One On Me
A Cuban string threesome
Playing nightly in Rio
Is referred to by the locals
As the fiddle Castro trio

Blown Over
You suck at the trumpet
Each time you try?
I think that is the
Reason why

Fighting Words
In the Middle Ages
Things were brutal
Perhaps because
Resistance was feudal

Off the Leash
I sought to learn of hunting dogs
Just how much do they weigh?
That is the reason I picked up
Some pointers yesterday

July Twentieth
1969
Neil and Buzz walk swiftly
On a sunny afternoon
When they were done they left behind
Their footprints on the moon

Circus clowns often socially diss tents

Nerve Wrecking
An ear worm bit my ear today
And I am quite annoyed
I cannot shake it from my head
It is a memoroid

Yes, Your Highness
Maui wowie - magic stuff
Joint smokers all exclaim it
It's not a term that I would use
"Coral Reefer" I would name it

Numb Feeling
Here at the nerve damage clinic
I love so very much
I'm afraid with many friends, it's true
I sadly have lost touch

Gee Mail
The saint of email?
Very easy
It is St. Francis
Of a cc

Up in Smoke
When my cow died
I was devastated
So I went out
And had her creamated

July Twenty First
1865
There certainly wasn't room enough
The two of them in one town
So Wild Bill Hickok killed Davis Tutt
In the first wild west showdown

Pigeons - we're talking bird banes

<u>Oh Dandy Boy</u>
Genghis Khan's half brother
An Irish paragon
Was someone people wouldn't touch
They called him Leper Khan

<u>Flee Bags</u>
Some women getting older
Seek ways to beat the blahs
They're fond of little tiny dogs
That have those mini paws

<u>Not a Rom-Com</u>
To help The Iliad
Get movie glory
They should call it
"Troy Story"

<u>Hook, Line, and Sinker</u>
That fly fish program
Is worthy of praising
Because, they say
The cast is amazing

<u>MD Headed</u>
Oh isn't it ironic how
A surgeon can amass
All the knowledge they require
Simply from cutting class

July Twenty Second
1967
Jimi Hendrix did his thing
But everyone agrees
He did it right by quitting from
Opening for the Monkees

Dog diseases can sometimes be heartworming

Maui Owie
I burned my Hawaiian pizza
But learned one thing for sure
Next time I'll set the oven on
Aloha temperature

Something's Fishy
Regarding my breath
I guess it's neurosis
That makes me think fish
Cause halibutosis

Artistic License
The art thieves worked
Quite fast, you know
When they went to grab
The Monet and Gogh

City Slicker
The butterfly sitting
Upon that cloth
Is just another
Urban moth

Rock and Roll
A sword in stone
Quite oversized
Would not come out
Til Arthurized

Kevin's Favorite Verses For Summer Days

July Twenty Third
1904
Charles Menches got the credit but
He didn't act alone
In serving up the very first
Ice cream cone

(More of) A Very Famous Restaurant

A Chinese option that they have
Is perfect, I maintain
To get it you must know that it
Is called the **Rob Lowe Mein**

If meat of cow instead you crave
The best choice you can make
Is sinking all your teeth into
Their **Mr. T Bone Steak**

Or perhaps a mix of exotic things
Is what appeals to you
If that's the case, then you should get
The **Eddie Rabbitt Stew**

Desserts are their great specialty
And I think that you'll see why
Try two, but let the first one be
Fiona Apple Pie

A second choice could be the most
Important one you'll make
Consider ordering a portion of
Darryl Strawberry Shortcake

If you prefer a simple one
Then leave it to the pros
And open up a package of
Some chocolate **Don Ho-hos**

July Twenty Fourth
1917
On trial as a spy
Refusing to say sorry
The Dutch exotic dancer
Known as Mata Hari

Elephant bathrooms require heavy doody cleaners

(More of) A Very Famous Restaurant

The best dessert is left to last
The price, though, very high
I think that it is justified
The **General Custard Pie**

For washing all this stuff along
You'll like what they have made
A concoction most delicious
That's called **Jack Lemmon Ade**

If citrus drink is not your style
With that hyperbole
I recommend you get yourself
Some **Peggy Lipton Tea**

And if nothing else works out for you
This last choice is a winner
Just go and microwave yourself
A **Gloria Swanson TV Dinner**

The Whelk

The whelk is a tasty gastropod
They eat in Rome and Florence
The one the U.S. knows, quite odd
Is simply known as Lawrence

Kevin's Favorite Verses For Summer Days

July Twenty Fifth
1999
The first of seven in a row
But it went oh so wrong
It was, of course, the steroid use
By cyclist Lance Armstrong

No Pain, No Gain
My personal trainer
Allows no excuse
Makes me do situps
So much ab use

Samsung, New Verse
I hear there's a new Galaxy phone
They claim it ranks a ten
But I just saw it and I'm afraid
It's the Samsung all over again

Latest Rankings
Regarding chicken, there only is
One thing you need to know
The Colonel's version is truly great
The General's, just Tso, Tso

Number Two Dries Harder
I'm happy to report here that
My brand new song is done
The name of it is "Tinkle" and
It's a surefire number one

Getting an Eiffel
In France, beware
Because at night
You may encounter
A Paris site

July Twenty Sixth
1775
Benjamin Franklin
On this day
Became Postmaster General
Of the USA

The smaller seesaw is the petiter totter

<u>Ego Media</u>
I think the two things mean the same
So you can take your pick
You can call it a device for selfies
Or a narcissist stick

<u>Over My Dead Body</u>
When I got a job in the hair salon
They asked me whether I
Had something I'd prefer to do
I said I'd rather dye

<u>Hard Working Peeple</u>
Internet urologists
Every time
Help us all
To stream online

<u>Filling the Bills</u>
Utilities are high
For water flowing
So prepare to be
H2Owing

<u>Thinking Ahead</u>
To be a reverse psychologist?
Oh how I would adore it
So I just told the manager
They shouldn't hire me for it

Kevin's Favorite Verses For Summer Days

July Twenty Seventh
1586
Sir Walter Raleigh
They should have said no
When you brought to England
The first tobacco

No Bull
The stockyard SWAT team
Tried something new
On arriving, yelled,
"POLICE - NOBODY MOO"

Footloose
A sock thief was arrested and
It could not be more shocking
They charged him with a single crime
And it, of course, was stocking

No Deposit
A case of soda fell on me
And gave me much alarm
Those twenty four containers, really
Caused me bottle-ee harm

Whine and Roses
You've got too much emotional baggage
It really is a waste
It seems to me you mostly are
Carrying a big griefcase

Happy Hooker
Captain Hook
For all to see
Ran his ship
Single-handedly

July Twenty Eighth
1933
Rudy Vallee
Quite the man
Received the first
Singing telegram

Great donut shop name - Amazing Glaze

Apologies to Richard Armour

Never shake a ketchup bottle
Nothing flows and then a lot'll
If you hit it in the middle
You will only get a little

And if you don't point
The end quite right
You will be become
A tomatic sight

So please remember
When you tilt
Which end is tapped
And which one's spilt

Krispy Kreme Dream

Last night I had a tasty dream
Of donuts made by Krispy Kreme
Deep fried circles all ablaze
Topped with a tasty sugary glaze

I distinctly remember requesting
To eat as things broke up
But then arose the hardest part
I woke up

Kevin's Favorite Verses For Summer Days

July Twenty Ninth
1927
If you had to have it
Its praises you sung
Today was the very first
Installed iron lung

My cow's phone has a mooed ring

Career Move
Yes, liposuction, I could do
That job is on my list
I really think that I would be
A great flabotomist

Looks are Deceiving
"I see an optical illusion"
I told my friend today
Turns out it really wasn't
It simply looked that way

Switched Off
A firefly had a problem big
This guy was quite short-sighted
One day he backed into a fan
Some say he was delighted

No Rough Edges
Pinocchio's shoes
Give him big frowns
Because they're just
Sand me downs

Will Full
A willed Stradivarius
The dead guy shares
Is certainly music
To his heirs

<u>Kevin's Favorite Verses For Summer Days</u>

July Thirtieth
2017
Computer hackers
In the know
Steal Games of Thrones
From HBO

<u>Mopping Up</u>
A dusty floor
Is a situation
Of suffering from
Sweep deprivation

<u>Soft Landing?</u>
My work as a hot air balloonist
Has left me with a frown
I lost that job, it's over now
I really let myself down

<u>Swede Dish</u>
A Scandinavian chef was shopping
And here is what he bought
Some Stockholm from the store so he
Could Sweden up the pot

<u>Going in Circles</u>
The Russians aimed way out in space
To make an orbit portal
They used it quite a while, but now
It's no place for Mir mortals

<u>Colonel Mustard</u>
OK, so maybe
I'm a cynic
But sick condiments need
The Mayo clinic

Kevin's Favorite Verses For Summer Days

July Thirty First
1922
Ralph Samuelson glided
O'er the water carefree
The very first person
To water ski

Hands Down
A naked man
In church was sought
And by the organ
He was caught

Necro Filly, Yeah
The undertaker's daughter
I'd say was rather
Odd because
Anyone cadaver

Tipping the Scales
40 pounds of skin, I'm told
I'll shed while getting older
Well that's good news because it is
A big weight off my shoulders

Writing Bug
My friend, an author in the medical field,
Created a giant schism
He wrote a book about black death
And was accused of plaguerism

A Big Hit
With marijuana legalized
We need pot drinks, I plead
Here is a tasty recipe
Ice, mocha, lotta weed

August First
1498
Columbus again
It was disclosed
Missed India again
At the Venezuelan coast

My bank account is suffering from cashtration

August Meditations

Motor homers pack all day
Cramming vans, driving away
These people really have odd zen
Getting away from it all
Means taking it with them

It isn't just for long vacations
That toys get brought along
Because right now in education
Technology sings its song

Papers, pencils, notebooks, rulers
Things once packaged up for schoolers
Now iPhones, Web and internet
Are what it seems each child must get

When school begins, this coming autumn
Modern parents will have bought 'em
And modern teachers too will find
That no iPad gets left behind

So thank you teachers, every one
We truly all are blessed
Although it wasn't always fun
I really can attest
That verses writ by fools like me
Began with learning ABCs

Kevin's Favorite Verses For Summer Days

August Second
1610
Henry Hudson
On this day
Went and discovered
His own bay

Live and Let Die
Sometimes I sit and wonder why
With no clue whatsoever
Like why do my hair cells have to die
But fat cells live forever?

Argggh
A pirate and woman fell in love
Don't ask, I don't know why
It didn't last too long because
They did not see aye to eye

Male Order
King Arthur's knights were picky
Their clothing, I contend
Was something that they purchased
From their favorite store - Lance End

A Bunch of Hose
The best firefighters
I could name
All got into
The Hall of Flame

Attendants Required
Flight training is
A situation
Where trainees get
Higher education

August Third
1936
Racing before Hitler
Jesse Owens was bold
Winning the first
Of his four medals gold

The toothless cow wanted to eat, but cudn't

Seas the Day
A sailing ship
Said some great wit
Is just one type of
Mast transit

Food Fight
That Red Lobster fight
Was quite the scare
Battered fish
Were everywhere

Bottled Up
When that Pepsi truck ran over me
I got upset and stressed
In fact, I'd go so far to say
That I was soda pressed

Nailed It
I heard this from
My buddy, Paul
If you've seen one sledge hammer
You've seen a maul

Psyched Out
I studied Freud all day and night
But have to be quite candid
I didn't really get it right
Too Jung to understand it

Kevin's Favorite Verses For Summer Days

August Fourth
1855
A wonderful payoff
After years of notation
John Bartlett published
"Familiar Quotations"

Bean There, Done That
I got food poisoned yesterday
There is no reason to doubt it
It was a Mexican restaurant
And I won't taco bout it

Telegraph Dot Com
Of Samuel Morse, I have to say
That I am quite a fan
There is a code that's named for him
He was a dashing man

Snail's Piece
The Daytona driver who won the race
Went out to eat, you know
To celebrate his victory
He ordered Nascargot

See Sickness
My sister is
A drama queen
So her doctor gave her
Melodramamine

BVDeeds
A thief in boxers
Lost the race
Police caught him
After a brief chase

<u>Kevin's Favorite Verses For Summer Days</u>

August Fifth
1884
To welcome tired, poor and hungry
Into their new home
The Statue of Liberty
Got its cornerstone

<u>Problem Solved</u>
The mathematician
Fixed a tough situation
By telling her ex
He's not part of the equation

<u>En-trance</u>
I bought a welcome mat of hemp
I'll give it here a plug
Although my buddy said to me
"Beware - it is a gateway rug"

<u>Fee Line</u>
I took my cat to the vet today
For its analysis
When I pointed out it didn't move
She said, "purralysis"

<u>Fast Forward Too</u>
My dog has just stopped moving
I do not know the cause
I simply noticed when he stood up
He seemed to be on paws

<u>On Dewty</u>
My steam powered phone
Has many faults
The worst of which
Are the mist calls

August Sixth
1926
In the English Channel
With confidence brimming
Gertrude Ederle made it
The first woman swimming

Foodie friends are taste buds

I've Had It With English (1)

I've had it with English
So please hear my rant
Why is there no egg
Inside an eggplant?

About a pineapple
I just have to whine
You won't find an apple
And there's no trace of pine

Plus in a hamburger
There's nary a gram
Of anything like
The meat of a ham

Fortunately, though
In this monologue
There's no trace of canine
Inside a hot dog

At big boxing rings
I can't help but swear
Because they're not round
Instead they are square

If a boxer can box
And a spammer can spam
Then how come a hammer
Is unable to ham?

August Seventh
1961
Nikita Kruschev
Had the nerve to suggest
That their economy
Would pass the U.S.

My new scarecrow is a no-brainer

I've Had It With English (2)

If a writer can write
And a singer can sing
Then what about fingers
Why can they not fing?

If you get in quicksand
Then you need to know
You will not sink quickly
In fact, it is slow

A nose might start running
Anytime you're unwell
But it's rather crazy
Your two feet can smell

If you should offend
A very good friend
You go make amends
Why not an amend?

If vegetarians eat vegetables
And shun all that meat
Please tell me then what should
Humanitarians eat?

You play at a recital
On a bright sunny day
So why do you then
Recite at a play?

Kevin's Favorite Verses For Summer Days

August Eighth
1974
After his duties
Had been forsaken
Nixon resigned
For the Watergate break-in

I've Had It With English (3)

You put cargo on ships
Paying many a buck
But if you go shipping things
They travel by truck

A slim chance and fat chance
Are the same, it's the pits
But wise men and wise guys
Are exact opposites

And what is the thinking
In this crazy town
Each house that burns up
Also burns down

If you should apply
To join the Cub Scouts
You'll fill in a form
By filling it out

And how does a colorfast
Fabric get done?
It sounds very speedy
But it will not run

These are all things
That my teachers have taught
I can't be a squeacher
Cuz I don't know squaught

August Ninth
1859
Though one wouldn't be built
Till many years later
A patent was issued
For the first escalator

A children's author is a kiddie litter

Pour Four
The Country Club dance
Held each year in their hall
Is a grand affair
One big golf ball

Style a While
Paris fashion week is here
The styles are all impressing
To me these are the salad days
Because they have French dressing

Saline, Saline
The President of Visine retired
A new one will be crowned
When he gave his going away speech
Not a dry eye could be found

Down the Drain
A plumbing apprentice works quite hard
To get the pipes all draining
He doesn't like descriptions, though
That say he's potty training

Steaks are High
Shipboard barbecues
Are very thrilling
Perhaps because of
Offshore grilling

Kevin's Favorite Verses For Summer Days

August Tenth
1889
Dan Rylands had
A bottle mishap
So he invented
The screw top cap

Double or Nothing
When the woman left
Her gambling hack
He went and tried
To win her back

Dino Might
If you fight dinosaurs
I would predict
You'll probably get
Jurassic kicked

Just Say No
The population needs to drop
To solve our planet's ills
Perhaps someone should give to it
Giant Earth control pills

Apple of her Eye
Eve's husband in the garden
Would not make time for squeezin'
So she was very mad at him
And for Adam good reason

LOL
I worry cuz my calendar
Is looking quite bereft
The days remaining in this week
Are written W-T-F

August Eleventh
1964
A zillion teenagers
Screamed and cheered
When "A Hard Day's Night"
In New York premiered

The pine's work was all for knot

Deter That Gent
A strange message
From a strange guy
"Soap making stuff missing"
"No lye"

Just a Pawn
In the big chess tournament
The players are neck and neck
I heard somewhere the winner
Always gets a check

Out of this World
Two extraterrestrials
Went and dated
When it came to their dinner
An alienated

The Pits
Conducting orchestras
He was quite slick at
The kind of thing
You shake a stick at

Fig Yours
When Eve changed clothes
'Twas rather brief
She'd just turn over
A brand new leaf

Kevin's Favorite Verses For Summer Days

August Twelfth
1930
Clarence Birdseye
A real chilling dude
Got a patent for inventing
Quick freezing food

Going to Pieces
I offer advice
To all of the masses
People in stone houses
Shouldn't throw glasses

High Pressure
Tiremakers never
Have a crisis
Selling at
Inflated prices

Pens Oil
My engine was very badly
Needing some protection
So I went and bought a book on lubes
From the non-friction section

Tenderizer
When Napoleon ate a chicken
That wouldn't come apart
He'd tug at it quite hard
To pull a Bonaparte

Chill in the Air
When Alaskan kids
Are unhappy at home
They pack their bags
And run away from Nome

August Thirteenth
1889
Though today it may seem
Rather quaint and quite funny
A phone patent permitted
Calls using money

<u>*Meat thieves are choplifters*</u>

<u>Oakey Dokey</u>
At Weyerhauser, I hear
It's hard to find seating
Whenever they have
A big board meeting

<u>Fools Russian In</u>
Though I know it's true for many foods
That Russians say 'nyet'
They all are happy eating pho
Cuz it is so Viet

<u>Rude Canal</u>
The army dentist
In his tent
Is the company
Drill sergeant

<u>Closing Costs</u>
Successful realtors
People say
Do one good deed
Every day

<u>De-tension</u>
A tardigrade is apropos
For a biology student lass
It's what the teacher gave to her
For being late for class

Kevin's Favorite Verses For Summer Days

August Fourteenth
1846
Thoreau took his protest
Up to the max
And got jailed for refusing
To pay up his tax

Curtain Time
A voting booth
In a political race
Is an election's
Mark-it place

Pulp Affliction
At paper conventions
It is a must
For important tissues
To be discussed

Flipper Off
I really love the dolphins
With them, I'm really thick
It's not so hard to understand
We all just seem to click

Strangely Arranged
Ripley's Believe it or Not
Dates back to the Victorian
And keeps all its stuff
In an odditorium

Roled Model
Getting made fun of
The actress didn't want
But this was her first play
And she got her debut taunt

August Fifteenth
1937
The Appalachian trail
An unbroken chain
2000 miles
From Georgia to Maine

When Apollo 13 failed to land on the moon, they sent Apollogies

A Tale of Two Fishies

*(published in Autumn Sky Poetry Daily - https://autumnskypoetrydaily.com/
2020/10/27/a-tale-of-two-fishies-by-kevin-ahern/*

Just yesterday I had a wish
To eat a little tunie fish

This dream of tasty albacore
Led me to my grocery store

Upon arriving on aisle three
I found my Chicken of the Sea

Or so I thought 'til I got back
And looked inside the grocery sack

Twas then I realized with terror
The grievous nature of my error

Beside the Reynolds cooking foil
Was tunie fish in cans of oil

I'll feed it to my Siamese
So I don't plug the arteries

Next time I go to shop I gotta
Buy tunie fish in cans of watta

Kevin's Favorite Verses For Summer Days

August Sixteenth
1896
Interest in the far north
Really spiked
With discovery of gold
In the Klondike

When my stomach got better, it was a big missed ache

At Least No Percussion
A musician's hurt
And cannot talk
While Chopin wood
He hurt his Bach

A Brush With the Aww
Here is my advice
I think that you should try it
When a front door has been painted
Don't knock it 'til you've dried it

Glooms Day
Though apocalypse
Would cause great sorrow
I joke of it
Like there's no tomorrow

Going Down
The movie music
From Titanic, I think
Is going to take
A while to synch

Like Dock Work
The longshoreman thinks
His boss is a jerk
Cuz he gets docked
When he shows up for work

August Seventeenth
1903
Joe Pulitzer
With journalistic ties
Donates a million bucks
For the Pulitzer prize

Of the two racetracks I own, one is the lesser of two ovals

No Bones
A tic-tac-toe board
So very fun
Is just an ex-oh
Skeleton

Doing Time
We're prisoners to the phone
And you can tell
That's why we say that
It's a cell

Barely Qualified
Out to a nudist colony
In the woods there by Big Sur
The newspaper sent a reporter
And a free glance photographer

Ounce of Prevention
I've thought a lot about drinking
And here I'll share my thoughts
If there's a vaccine I'm needing
I'm ready to take my shots

Gone, but Forgotten
A rich guy is dead
Who he is, no one knows
The police are now referring to him
As Mister John Dough

Kevin's Favorite Verses For Summer Days

August Eighteenth
1912
The mayor of Tokyo
Liking what he sees
Gives Washington, DC
2000 cherry trees

Van White
I bought a Honda minivan
It is a bunch of fun
Has everything I wanted
You Odyssey it run

Kent Lucky
Superman and his gal pal
Solely of their own volition
Just went out and had themselves
A Lois and Clark expedition

Numbers Game
Our chicken business went and hired
Another new accountant
Who warns us, "Don't hatch your chicks"
"Until they're counted"

Social Meet Ya
Marijuana shops
Like it when
Their customers
Reefer a friend

Strong Scent
Cross a skunk with a dog
It's not that hard
If you do, you'll get
A scent Bernard

August Nineteenth
2008
Critics mostly
Seemed to be pleased
When Lady Gaga's first album
Got released

Forgetful cows give milk of amnesia

The One That Got a Weigh
The fisherman's claim
"Big as a whale"
Means he caught fish
By the tale

Hot Dog!
The food critic showed
Casual demeanor
Proclaiming that
"Oscar Mayer is a wiener"

Won't Fly
A new rule has been put in place
For archery club members now
You're in trouble on induction
If you should take a bow

Dead On
Amazing sights
If you go see 'em
All the dead rodents
In the new mouseleum

Punching Big
The boxing match
Began with ease
Thanks to opening
Fistivities

Kevin's Favorite Verses For Summer Days

August Twentieth
1882
In Moscow, a symphony
Majestic for sure
Tchaikosky's
1812 Overture

<u>Ummmmm</u>
The umbrella inventor
Thought it might have allure
If she could call it 'brella'
But sadly wasn't sure

<u>Real Cut-Ups</u>
Buying Norwegian chopping tools
Is money quite well-spent
I love the way that each one smells
Can't beat a foreign axe scent

<u>Hard Slider</u>
I'm very sorry now to report
That Mr. Drake has passed
After he was covered in lard
He went downhill quite fast

<u>Shocking</u>
No current license?
You won't go far
If you possess
An electric car

<u>Ups and Downs</u>
Elevator music
Is made by devils
Annoying at
Many levels

August Twenty First
1858
Who knew the drama
These two would create?
The first of several
Lincoln-Douglas debates

Breakfast Shakespeare is a Hamlet

After Taste
Artificial sweeteners
Your praises they sing
Cuz love is a many
Splenda thing

Bottoms Up
My butt nerves - gone
And I'm delirious
No laughing, cuz I'm
Dead ass serious

Irreplaceable at the Joint
The guy at the marijuana shop
Is serving as the clerk
He puts in 20 hours per week
Doing pot time work

Shocking News
An electrician is in trouble
The local news reports
Apparently he's been fiddling
With other people's shorts

Making Change
A bunch of big pink flowers
Fell out of the sky May seven
The logical explanation?
'Twas raining peonies from heaven

August Twenty Second
1902
Thinking it might
Help him go far
Teddy Roosevelt became
The first Prez to ride in a car

Lechers like belle bottoms

The Realtor

My realtor friend
Just likes to say
She does a good deed
Every day

And she's the one
To go and find
If you've a lot
On your mind

Too Much Time

*(published in the inaugural issue of Flight of the Dragonfly - https://
flightofthedragonfly.com/ kevin-ahern/)*

I got arrested the other day
Seems what I did was not OK

An officer told me that my crime
Was I had taken too much time

"But what," I said, "I didn't know"
"That it was time for me to go"

"Ignorance," he said, "is no excuse"
"You mess with time and you will lose"

Because of this, it seems that I'm
A person who'll be doing time

August Twenty Third
1962
A way for broadcasts
To travel far
Europe and American
Celebrate Telstar

When the Chinese cook got injured, the doctor said he may never wok again

Life Lines
With respect to getting older
I told my buddy, Max
What you see may look like wrinkles
But really, they're just wise cracks

Up on the Roof Top
My chimney jokes are popular
From Mexico to Laos
I give them all away for free
Because, you see, they're on the house

On the Mend
The news about the sick bear's health
Just reached us from the vet
It seems he's doing better, but
He's not out of the woods just yet

Leveled Off
Kansans are a
Hearty band
Living off
The flat of the land

Senior Citizen
The slowest gun
In the West you'd see
Was the guy they called
Wyatt A-A-R-P

Kevin's Favorite Verses For Summer Days

August Twenty Fourth
1853
Eaten at
A furious clip
George Crum makes
The first potato chip

<u>Curdsy</u>
Miss Muffett's book
Is out today
The title of it?
"Around About Whey"

<u>Foot Loose, Fiancé Free</u>
One young college student I know
Says he always wants to be free
He's avoiding marriage so strongly that
They gave him a Bachelor's degree

<u>It Will Be Held Against Me</u>
I know an expert in cell phone law
Its intricacies she can decode
Apparently if your phone gets charged
It has the right to remain in silent mode

<u>Blow-hard</u>
Expelling air to voice frustration
Makes folks around me scatter
It seems to work - I get my way
Which I guess must mean sighs matter

<u>Real Cut Up</u>
Sir Lancelot
It would appear
Had a sworded affair
With Guinevere

<u>Kevin's Favorite Verses For Summer Days</u>

August Twenty Fifth
1609
Glowing with pride
Over his creation
Galileo performed
His telescope demonstration

<u>Push!</u>
For birthing now
Without a doubt
Midwives really
Help people out

<u>Bubbly Personality</u>
I gave tonic water
To my girl last week
That's how I Schwepped her
Off her feet

<u>Gone With the Wind</u>
I have some news
That's sad to share
The balloon family died out
When there was no heir

<u>Tomorrow, Tomorrow</u>
A friend said I won't go far
Because I procrastinate
But I got the last word when I said,
"Just you wait"

<u>A Shoe-in</u>
The alligator's feelings
Are very heartfelt
He's proud of the fact
His son's a black belt

Kevin's Favorite Verses For Summer Days

August Twenty Sixth
1947
Don Bankhead made
Two baseball stats
The first black pitcher
And a homer in his first at bat

Sum Game
"That Fibonacci joke,"
The math guy opined,
"Is as bad as the last two"
"You've told, combined"

Up in Smoke
If you ban flavored cigarettes
Then I will truly kiss you
Those awful things that make smoke rings
Are menthol health issues

Need to Let Go
In the obituaries today
I was very sad to see
The Velcro inventor passed away
R-I-P

Lactose Tolerant
I think I am addicted
To dairy, for goodness sakes
Cuz each attempt I make to stop
Results in more milk shakes

Burning Sensation
When it comes to death
This is no bull
All men are truly
Cremated equal

August Twenty Seventh
2008
Today there was
A political precedent
First African American
Nominated for President

Drummers are very cymbal minded

<u>Bullions of Dollars</u>
When I was in Jamaica
I couldn't believe my seein'
That they had lots of fools' gold
Pyrites of the Caribbean

<u>Count On It</u>
When I learned of my Transylvanian roots
It caused in me great fear
So bad that to this day I can't
Look myself in the mirror

<u>Winning the Lottery</u>
A nose has entered the raffle
Cuz something inside just "clicked"
He saw that by buying tickets
There was a good chance he'd be picked

<u>Game Over</u>
Super Mario players
Can't be ignored
If they talk to the dead
With a Luigi board

<u>Groovy</u>
When LPs die
It is the case
They go to their vinyl
Resting place

Kevin's Favorite Verses For Summer Days

August Twenty Eighth
1845
Today it still
Is a big success
Scientific American
Rolled off the press

No Beef About It
When Porky Pig
Mysteriously died
The sheriff called it
Hamicide

Earrings
The Tinnitus Help line's
Light is blinking
I hear their phone
Will not stop ringing

Not a Perk
I hit my head on the coffee pot
And it left me quite confused
I worry each time I use it now
Cuz it gives nasty brews

Brush with the Awe
When it comes to modern painting
It's Picasso I prefer
All the things he puts on canvas
Strokes of genius, yes they were

Not a Pushover
That tightrope walker over there
Seems oh so awfully young
For someone who most always is
Terribly high strung

August Twenty Ninth
1896
Not quite where
You'd expect it to be
Chop Suey invented
In NYC

Potatoes that turn against you are traitor tots

Thinking of You

A flower in
A forest grew
Its color no one
Ever knew

The form it took
We do not know
How long it lived
Where did it grow?

If there's no ears
When elm trees fall
It's said they make
No sound at all

For flowers of which
I've never thought
Did they exist?
Some say they'd not

But you exist
I know it's true
Because I'm always
Thinking of you

Bats

A mother bat with little pups
Teaches them the downside ups
One fact of them nobody knows
When they drop stuff, which way it goes

Kevin's Favorite Verses For Summer Days

August Thirtieth
1972
A really amazing
Flipping nut
The gold awarded
To Olga Korbut

Up Close
I really want
To watch cells do it
A microscope?
I'll look into it

Under Wares
To steal a person's
BVDs
A thief goes on
Brief crime sprees

No-Brainer
The zombie apocalypse is coming
'Twill be the next big wave
They're seeking out good brains to eat
Relax, my friend, you're safe

Deep Dish
At the Vatican, the eats improved
And I think I know why
It seems they now are serving up
Poperoni pizza pie

Soaking It Up
An underwater marriage
Is something you shouldn't miss
Cuz in it you see a couple
Experiencing wetted bliss

August Thirty First
1925
With her Samoan studies
On coming of age
Margaret Meade
Was all the rage

I'm the charman of our bar-b-Q group

Last Gasp
The view in space
There is no faking
With helmet off
It's quite breathtaking

Spectrum Disorder
When it comes to diet
They're great big cheaters
Black holes' thin-ness
Comes from being light eaters

Horn Guy
Herbie the Love Bug's gotten old
A bunch of rusting chrome
He lives with other Beetles now
Down at the old Volks home

Milking It
A dairy flinging contest doesn't
Happen every day
To some it is important
To me, it's a throw a whey

Numb and Number
Here's a weird circumstance
Creating many woes
Whenever your foot goes to sleep
You've got comatoes

Kevin's Favorite Verses For Summer Days

September First
1904
Radcliffe College
Anxiously awaited
When Helen Keller
Graduated

Off Beat
I love to tell police jokes
So many I've expressed
I've heard a few complaints of late
So I'll give it arrest

A Tangled Web
Hair conditioner users
Of which there sure are lots
Can be divided into
The haves and the have knots

Unique Perspective
I met an endoscopist
And now I'm really primed
Cuz she told me she would
Look me up sometime

Dead Head
The guy working at
The crematorium burned it
When he got promoted
He truly urned it

Running On
An offending semi-colon
Must now do penance
For this they gave him
Consecutive sentences

<u>Kevin's Favorite Verses For Summer Days</u>

September Second
1992
The U.S. and Russia
On this occasion
Agree to build
A space station

<u>Blue Ribbon</u>
The judge's house
That she just bought
Has won a prize
Honorable mansion it got

<u>On the Run</u>
A hacker escaped
From police today
The rumor was
He went data way

<u>Anatomically Correct</u>
The search for two armed men
Set off some strange alarms
Cuz everybody that I know
Has two arms

<u>Taking Orders</u>
The waitress' work
Is rather stable
It's not much fun
But it puts food on the table

<u>Wedding Vowels</u>
Old man MacDonald and his wife
Renewed their vowels, you know
When they did it in their ceremony
They said E-I-E-I-O

Kevin's Favorite Verses For Summer Days

September Third
1838
Disguised as a sailor
Exhibiting bravery
Frederick Douglass
Escapes slavery

Librated
Your obsession with astrology
Was not so smart
In fact I think I'd say
It Taurus apart

Unbalanced Beaming
A gymnast got arrested
For breaking into cars
For ten years she was sentenced
Behind parallel bars

Not for Checkout
The librarian's left him
All unhooked
When he asked for a date
She said she was booked

The Price Ain't Right
To the auction they went
With keen intent
But ended up with
Bidder disappointment

Kiss of Life
OK, here's the latest
On the insect situation
After it hit the porch light
It got moth to moth resuscitation

September Fourth
1951
For the first time there
Everyone could see
A transcontinental broadcast
On TV

When James Bond takes a bath, it's bubble 07

Dis Stilled
And back in France
It's really odd
Their holy water
Is "Eau, my god"

Instru Mental
The musician went
And broke a rule
Pulling strings
To pass harp school

To Your Health
In Holland, "Bottoms up"
Means more than just good cheer
In fact, the loose translation is
"Your Heineken drink Dutch beer"

Spicy Language
Two chefs arguing
Made such an awful sound
The subject for discussion?
Finding cumin ground

Inclining Amphibian
That very young frog
Has spring in his walk
The guy's been invited
To give a TAD Talk

Kevin's Favorite Verses For Summer Days

September Fifth
1889
Upholding principles
Near and dear
Christine Hardt
Patents the brassiere

Diss Engagement
Though he may have a license
A wedding he dismisses
Cuz a bachelor is a hunter
Who simply never Mrs.

Self Medication
The Acupuncture Help line
Is at it again
It requires you to login
And enter a PIN

A Brine of the Times
I got in a pickle the other day
And had a conniption fit
My wife said it didn't matter much
And told me to dill with it

Frosted Over
To try to deal with
A bruise from a hit
The gingerbread man
Tried icing it

Movie Buzz
That honey making video
Is really groovy
Highly recommended
A good bee movie

<u>Kevin's Favorite Verses For Summer Days</u>

September Sixth
1916
Charles Saunders
Hit it bigly
With the first supermarket
Piggly Wiggly

<u>Seeing Through Someone</u>
I hate to say your friend's a ghost
And cause a big uproar
But I realized that it was true
The minute she walked through the door

<u>Kook Out</u>
Notable for
Its unusual schema
My Brazilian bar-b-q
Is the grill from Ipanema

<u>Prime Choice</u>
A vegan that I had in class
Impressed me, I must say
Though her performances was impeccable
Was it wrong to give her Grade A?

<u>Down Under</u>
The Aussies have
Unusual ways
Of celebrating
Their Perth days

<u>Aroma Wasn't Built . . .</u>
The expensive perfume
She wears to events
Suggests that lady
Has no common scents

Kevin's Favorite Verses For Summer Days

September Seventh
1909
Eugene Lefebvre
Made his name
The first pilot dying
In an airplane

Phone Follies

I was feeling blue just yesterday
Til I dialed a corporation
The automated voice I got
Began a conversation

Its perky tone raised up my hopes
A modern techno gem
It told me that my call was very
Important to all of them

And that feeling of importance soared
With the voice's reassurance
That my call would be recorded for
Quality assurance

I guess they think me knowledgeable
In all the words I say
My spirits buoyed I walked around
On a cloud the rest of the day

There's just one thing that puzzles me
And it is rather strange
Why is it every time I call
The menu options change?

September Eighth
1504
A naked man
Was unveiled
The Statue of David
Immediately hailed

Swedish dogs bjark

Mind Games
I hit my head upon a drum
Creating much discussion
The opinion of the doctor was
I might have a percussion

Looking at the Stars
The tent insurance I just bought
Is lacking, I've discovered
Cuz if my gear gets stolen
I simply won't be covered

Wrong Key
When the cellist's sound
Came out quite flat
The conductor said,
"Why in the F did you do that?

Bedex?
A postal carrier
I do report
Is a special kind
Of mail escort

Comeback
An impressive retort
Was made in the spring
Some said it was
Quite a May zing

Kevin's Favorite Verses For Summer Days

September Ninth
1543
Mary Stuart
On the scene
Nine months old
And crowned the queen

<u>Your Eyes Say Yes, Yes, Yes</u>
The lady was ready
With her boyfriend to "do it"
He said "No protection"
But she condom into it

<u>Snooze Blues</u>
Please be quiet
Do not shout
I'm up in the top bunk
Over and out

<u>Kiss of Death</u>
My wife taught me well
I've now got the smarts
She awarded me a black belt
In marital arts

<u>Corny</u>
I ask you, please
Give me a pardon
For defining vegetables
As what scarecrows are garden

<u>Cough It Up</u>
The Heimlich Hotel's the kind of place
That you should not be dodging
Among its many services
Are excellent food unlodging

September Tenth
2008
The Large Hadron Collider
Is finally transformed
The most expensive collisions
Earthlings performed

Spanish postal carriers are from Parcelona

Seeing Things Through
Inside the dictionary
I hear
The meaning of opaque
Is most unclear

Glow in the Dork
Mood rings are great
Who can resist 'em?
They're really good for serving
As early warning systems

Plane Killers
When it's time to fly south
For mallards and drakes
Many are afflicted
With migrate headaches

Slow Learner
My knowledge of mythology
Of the Greeks is to me
Something I recognize
As my Achilles knee

"And Don't Come Back"
The door closing contest
In Amsterdam
Concludes today
With the grand slam

Kevin's Favorite Verses For Summer Days

September Eleventh
1847
It was today
The catchy tune
O Susannah!
Debuted in a Pittsburgh saloon

<u>Classic Rock</u>
I found a new book on tribute bands
Of which I am a lover
I spent the weekend reading it
Cover to cover to cover

<u>Unspeakable</u>
My friend, the mime, has quit his job
Despite a strong devotion
The reason was he felt that he
Was just going through the motions

<u>Punctuated Relationship</u>
When two copy editors socialize
If they have their druthers
They'll get a dinner, movie too
And, uh comma date each other

<u>Random Tweet</u>
Birds are better off
I guess
At pursuing life, liberty
And happy nests

<u>Bottoms Up</u>
A cheer was shouted
By the tavern door
"One tequila, two tequila"
"Three tequila, floor"

September Twelfth
1873
Many would use it
To tell their tale
The first practical typewriter
Was available for sale

My unfinished novel is a half-booked idea

<u>Dearly Departed</u>
A major shipment disappeared
At a very serious cost
Police are combing the area where
The truck of wigs was lost

<u>Done With the Wind?</u>
I'm writing a poem about the wind
Of which my good friend laughed
I told her that it wasn't done
And still was just a draft

<u>Coded Message</u>
I got a big apology
To which I had been owed
'Twas written in dots and dashes, though
Some kind of remorse code

<u>Jolly Roger</u>
The person to whom
You should focus your ire at
Is the lunch box thief
A chicken pot pirate

<u>On Top of It</u>
Your adulterous acts
Are quite astounding
You'll get caught
Evidence is mounting

Kevin's Favorite Verses For Summer Days

September Thirteenth
1907
The Lusitania
With record ways
Crosses the Atlantic
In just five days

<u>Foreign Relations</u>
The Mexican cousin
Of Tinkerbell
Is someone known
As Taco Bell

<u>Making Their Marks</u>
Engravers always work quite hard
Unless their work is thwarted
And if that happens they will be
Etching to get started

<u>Viet Nom Nom</u>
A Vietnamese restaurant that never closes
Makes me feel like heaven
Its name is very apropos
They call it Twenty Pho Seven

<u>Fathom of the Opera</u>
To an underwater opera
Italians all say "Viva!"
They need to find a singer, though
Perhaps a scuba diva?

<u>Eggsactly</u>
Some say menstrual cramps
Cause too much reacting
A classic case
Of ovary acting

September Fourteenth
1814
Francis Scott Key
Saw bombs burst in air
And wrote up an anthem
About a flag still up there

Candy for positive people - Encourage Mints

No Fee?
When Jack climbed up the beanstalk
He got up very high
But couldn't reach the Internet
So he asked the Giant, "Why Fi?"

A Certive
If you ask me, I'd truly say
Tic Tacs are for the birds
But yes, I really do prefer
Not to mints words

Arachnophilia
Do not buy pet store spiders
No matter what they said
There are much cheaper sources
Try looking on the Web

Mouthful
When her feather pillow
Had a leak
She got down in the mouth
For about a week

Tummy Time
As for any battle
Napoleon could win it
And making his coat?
He had a hand in it

Kevin's Favorite Verses For Summer Days

September Fifteenth
1928
Recognizing
Bacterial killin'
Alexander Fleming
Discovers penicillin

Rationing
Two roosters per man
I say to you
Are just too many
A cock a dude'll do

Straight Talk
I communicate with whiskey
To me it really talks
We have a relationship that is
Always on the rocks

Feline Lines
Morris, my cat, talks up a storm
The veterinarian swears
One day when Morris said "meow"
The doctor asked him, "where?"

Barking Up the Right Tree
Down at the pound, my dog was found
And sent back home to me
Another demonstration of
Excellent collar ID

Lunar Cycle
Each time a mermaid
Smiles too wide
You notice that
She gets tongue tide

September Sixteenth
1997
As the computer industry
Slowly burns
Steven Jobs
To Apple returns

Maids are weapons of muss destruction

The Little Kitty

I found a little kitty
It followed me one day

I had a lot of fun with it
I loved to watch it play

My laser light astounded it
A ball of yarn it chased

The world was one big mystery
That cat was so amazed

And all was well until today
While playing with some socks

The little kitty fell into
A rather largish box

That folded up and closed itself
The kitten deep inside

Perhaps it's happy in the fact
It has a place to hide

Or maybe it has perished
Just one way to decide

Damn you Schrödinger

Kevin's Favorite Verses For Summer Days

September Seventeenth
1683
van Leeuwenhoek's new
Microscope tool
Shows him bacteria
He dubs "animalcules"

Dirty Joke
When Maggie Thatcher slipped in mud
The headline writers roiled
For earning herself the status as
"The Greatest Tory Ever Soiled"

Plank Constant
A sad lumberyard accident
Attributed to meth
Turned out to have a different cause
He was just board to death

Double Letter Score
A lady got a message that
Quite deeply did upset her
It seems the Scrabble company
Sent her a threatening letter

From Cost to Cost
My boating expenses
Will soon be slipping
I just bought one online
And it came with free shipping

Doesn't Add Up
Plants don't count
When planting fruits
Cuz doing math
Gives them square roots

September Eighteenth
1851
The New York Times
Did this day commence
Its publishing
The cost? Two cents

Extraterrestrial painters say "Take me to your ladder"

Your Castle or Mine?
Medieval maidens had their fun
And screamed out with delight
Some carried it to great extremes
Each and every knight

Unbalanced Act
The Russian acrobat pyramid team
From competing has withdrawn
It seems they have a problem cuz
They don't have Oleg to stand on

Sore Spot
I dropped a six pack on my foot
But that's not the worst of the news
Because the place it landed on
Is covered now with brews

Control Issue
I need the TV controller
To change the station
I'm guessing it is sitting
In a remote location

Horse Sense
Down at the online horse store
They tell you at the start
If you find one you like a lot
Then "Add it to your cart"

Kevin's Favorite Verses For Summer Days

September Nineteenth
1970
She could "light the world up with her smile"
And rode it to great success
The Mary Tyler Moore Show
Premiered on CBS

Moving Target
A recent writing experience
Turned into quite a caper
I wrote a book on cats for it
But should have just used paper

Taco Bull
Cuisine from south of the border
Deserves its share of hype
So if you do not like this food
Then I am nacho type

Continental Rift
If you are studying geology
Then please remember this
To practicing geologists
Igneous is bliss

Still Lying Down
A famous napper died last week
His tombstone had one wrinkle
The only message it contained
Was R.I.P Van Winkle

Going Postal
The postal worker's work
Is suddenly much better
Because she knows that she can do
Whatever the boss will letter

September Twentieth
1973
A victory for women
Over a chauvinist pig
Billy Jean King
Defeats Bobby Riggs

Cat veterinarians are purramedics

School of Hard Knacks
Here's my advice
'Twould be wise to heed it
Experience you get
Only after you need it

Silence is Golden
If you've nothing smart to say
Here's my advice, please try it
You're never ever gonna be wrong
By simply keeping quiet

Social Distancing
Louisiana is for loners
I heard it from an elf
Cuz you can go there any time
And be all bayou self

Deafinitely
I gave up on my ear doctor
Cuz he has such bad zen
He told me I was going deaf
And I never heard from him again

Having Contractions
Though I'm getting old
I know for sure
The diff between
Your and you're

Kevin's Favorite Verses For Summer Days

From the Author

I'm an odd guy - a Professor Emeritus from Oregon State University (Biochemistry/Biophysics) who loves to write things that make people laugh and think.

Besides books of verses, I'm a co-author on three biochemistry textbooks. I also write other fun things, like song lyrics I call Metabolic Melodies. The Melodies initially were solely about biochemical processes and I sang them to my classes, but when I started running out of biochemistry topics, I switched to writing song lyrics about things like the Oregon weather, politics, and other topics I was interested in.   I have over 200 of these at my Web site.

For six years, I wrote a new limerick every day and they are collected in some of the books listed below (all book info is at my Web site - www.davincipress.com). When the limerick format got old, I started writing short verses and then moved on to longer ones.

Some of my books:

1. The Odd Farmers' Almanac for 2022 (2021 also)
2. A Limerick a Day for a _____ Year (first, second, third, fourth, fifth, sixth)
3. My Many Merry Melodies
4. The Complete Irks of Kevin Ahern
5. Biochemistry (Mathews, van Holde, and Ahern)
6. Biochemistry Free and Easy (Ahern and Rajagopal)
7. Biochemistry Free for All (Ahern, Rajagopal, and Tan)
8. Kevin and Indira's Guide to Getting Into Medical School

Besides writing, I also have hundreds of biochemistry video lectures in various places - URLs below

1. **The Great Courses** - https://www.thegreatcourses.com/courses/ biochemistry-and-molecular-biology-how-life-works
2. **Lecturio** - https://app.lecturio.com/#/course/c/8060
3. **YouTube Channel** - https://www.youtube.com/user/oharow

I also have an audio series of lectures on how to get into Medical school at Listenable - https://listenable.io/web/courses/143/kevin-aherns-guide-to-getting-into-medical-school/

I love to hear from fans. I'm on Facebook (kevin.g.ahern) and Twitter (@ahernk1.). Also, as noted above, my Web page is at www.davincipress.com